Millie's Library Card

By

R. G. Patrick

®

AuthorHouse™
1663 Liberty Drive
Bloomington, IN 47403
www.authorhouse.com
Phone: 1 (800) 839-8640

This book is printed on acid-free paper.

ISBN: 978-1-7283-2156-1 (sc)
ISBN: 978-1-7283-2157-8 (e)

Library of Congress Control Number: 2019910705

Print information available on the last page.

Published by AuthorHouse 07/30/2019

authorHOUSE®

Dedication

This book is dedicated to my sons, Gathon and Loren. Their unconditional love and the joys they bring enable me to laugh out loud! Their childhood joys coupled with my childhood imaginations have help establish the foundation for Millie Jacobson!

I Love You Both so very dearly.

Thank you for being you!

Preface

Millie's world is a replication of the childhood imaginations and friendships established while growing up in the 70's. Getting a first library card was a huge accomplishment growing up! The joy of reading has never left me! Expansion of the imagination is accomplished through reading. Reading can take you places of which you may not have dreamt. I am hopeful that the many adventures of Millie Jacobson will bring you as much joy as it brings me to introduce her! Look forward to many more events!

illie leapt out of bed! "It's here!" she squealed. "Saturday is here!" Millie could not get into her robe and slippers fast enough. She must hurry. Millie wanted to be the first one at the Library when it opened! Today is the day to get her first independent reader, library card! With this card, Millie can borrow books from the library on her own without Momma or Papa's help

Millie raced down the hall with her pink ruffled robe flying behind. Her slippers were barely on her feet as she slid to a stop just behind her favorite seat at the table in their small kitchen. Millie gathered herself and quietly slid the chair back just enough to sit close to the table. Millie knew better than to make too much ruckus. Momma enjoyed quiet on Saturday and Sunday mornings especially before getting up for a weekend shift. She and Papa worked very hard on weekdays. However, Momma would occasionally take extra hours on the weekend.

"Princess, what's your rush? Is there a bee in your bonnet this morning?" asked Papa with a wide grin as he poured cereal into Millie's bowl. He knew that Millie was excited about the library card. Millie went to the library the second Saturday of each month! Ever since her first awareness of such a place, Millie could not be contained. Papa loved to see Millie and TJ excited about life. Millie and her brother, TJ, are twins and the best of Friends!

"Oh, Papa! I'm not wearing a bonnet!" Millie giggled. "Today is Saturday! Today I get my own library card! Don't you remember?"

Papa stopped with the breakfast preparations, tilted his head to one side, and looked inquisitively to the ceiling as if in deep thought. "Are you sure it is today?" Papa asked jokingly.

"Papa!" Squealed, Millie. "Of course it is today! Yesterday was Friday. So, today is Saturday!"

Papa laughed gently and said, "I know, Princess. Just checking." Papa continued with the breakfast preparation adding milk to Millie's cereal.

"Not too much, Papa. It will get too wet." Cautioned Millie. Millie knew that she did not really have to remind Papa. He made every breakfast just right.

"Well, here comes my Shadow!" Papa said joyfully as TJ entered the room still rubbing sleep from his eyes. TJ did not like getting up in the mornings. But, he made an exception for Saturdays! TJ knew that getting up early on Saturday meant that he would get through with his chores sooner and have much more playtime outside with his friends. TJ was looking forward to today's street ball games. He knew that if he got outside early enough he would be one of the Captains. If not, he would at lease get the chance to get picked early enough. Playing on a team was not ever a concern for TJ. He ran faster than most of the kids in the neighborhood even some of the bigger kids.

Papa always referred to TJ as his shadow. They spent a lot of time together doing 'Guy Stuff'. TJ enjoyed spending time with Papa as much as he enjoyed playing street ball! "Morning, Papa." Said a rather sleepy TJ.

"Good Morning to you too, Shadow!" Papa always appeared to be in a good mood in the mornings. TJ liked that about Papa. He knew how to make TJ feel that no matter what, today is starting off to something great!

Papa poured TJ's favorite cereal. "You do remember our special event today; don't you TJ?""

Of course!" said TJ with a mouth full of cereal. "Today, we get a library card! Then, I can borrow books on my own!" TJ was excited about the opportunity to get his action books all on his own! He and his friends would read and imagine themselves as superheroes! With his own library card, TJ will have the opportunity to get the books before his friends! Now, he will not have to wait for Papa or Momma to get books from the library!

"Slow down there, Shadow!" said, Papa "We have plenty of time before the library opens. You have time to chew your food." Papa had to laugh. He enjoyed seeing the excitement in his children when it comes to education. Papa and Momma loved school as children and encouraged a healthy approach to education with Millie and TJ. Papa and Momma were first generation college graduates. Even though Papa's was a junior college, it allowed him the chance to advance further than his parents. He and Momma wanted more for Millie and TJ and the joy of reading was the best start!

TJ and Millie cleared their bowls from the table and ran to their rooms to get dressed. Millie and TJ were responsible for keeping their rooms and their bathroom in order each day. Papa and Momma said that it was to teach them how to be responsible and respect the home. Each day that they accomplished their chores, gave them points that they could use to request an extra Birthday or Christmas gift. Millie was much more consistent than TJ with earning points. TJ just did not seem to care as much about a neatly made bed.

TJ was ready before Millie, as usual, so he collected each of their library books from the family library and waited in the living room for Papa and Millie. Millie arrived first. She and TJ started a game of checkers as they waited for Papa. Millie was determined to win best two out of three! TJ was the checker champion! She just had to win! They were on their second game when Papa came downstairs! "Papa! I can win this round!" exclaimed Millie. Millie needed to win this round to stay in the game. TJ had already won the first round!

"Okay." Said Papa. He sat down to watch. There it was! TJ's winning move! He did not take it! Papa was both surprised and impressed. TJ purposefully choose a move that would leave Millie with the chance to win! Millie took the move and won the second round!

"Papa! I won! TJ missed a move! Did you see that Papa? I won round two!" Millie was super excited!

"I did see that, Millie. Now, it's time to go to the library, you two. TJ did you get all of the books that we borrowed last week?"

TJ replied, "Yes, Papa."

"Thank you, TJ." Papa said with a wink to TJ. TJ winked back. He realized from the wink that Papa knew what he had done. TJ and Millie grabbed their outerwear and books and headed for the door.

Once they stepped outside, Papa took each child by the hand and they headed down the block to the library. The majestic building was the beacon of adventure for Millie and TJ! They stood on the corner waiting for the traffic signal to turn green before crossing. They each chattered about the books they wanted to get first with their library cards! "Look, Millie! There it is! I can't wait to get the next Batman before Michael James! He will have to read it after me!" TJ was super excited. Millie stood in silence admiring the architecture of the building full of magic and imagination!

They crossed the street with Papa and climbed the steps to the library. As they entered the library, Millie could smell that comforting aroma of book pages and floor wax. The chemicals used to clean the wood and marble floors of the library were both familiar and relaxing. They approached the front desk. Papa spoke to the Librarian first. "Good morning, Ms. Margaret. How are you feeling today?"

Ms. Margaret looked up from her reading just above the top rim of her glasses. " Good morning, Mr. Jacobson! I am doing well! How are you?" Ms. Margaret was familiar with the Jacobson family. They came every Saturday morning. Sometimes it was Mr. Jacobson with the twins, Millie and TJ. Other times, it was Mrs. Jacobson with the twins. Ms. Margaret enjoyed seeing the neighborhood families using the local library services.

"We are doing very well!" Papa responded. "We are here for new library cards! Millie and TJ are ready to get their first library card!"

Ms. Margaret gave a bright smile. "Well, there is nothing more exciting than that! Are you two ready for the responsibility?" asked Ms. Margaret.

"Yes!" exclaimed Millie and TJ in unison.

"Okay." said Ms. Margaret. Then she proceeded to gather the papers for signatures and information pamphlets to take home. Ms. Margaret explained the rules of the library for cardholders and users. The twins paid close attention. Papa signed a couple of documents and then it happened! Millie and TJ were each given a sheet to sign next to Papa's signature and then signed each of their library cards! For a moment Millie's mind went blank. She could not remember what books she wanted to get first. Then she remembered that she had made a list with Momma's help and the list was in her purse.

   "Papa! Let's go look for my books!" Exclaimed Millie. Millie took Papa by the hand and led the way to the Children's Book section of the library. TJ was right behind. He kept looking at his library card. TJ was super excited. Now, he had something to put in his wallet besides a few baseball cards. TJ slid his library card into a identification slot of his wallet so that each time he opened his wallet, he could see the library card through the plastic window. TJ also had a list that Momma had helped him prepared. His list was on a folded slip of paper in the billfold compartment of his wallet. They all stopped at the card catalogue desk. Here is where the search for books began. Papa said that the library used a filing system called Dewey Decimal. Papa said that it was a widely used method of classification that allowed for easy sorting of materials. In this case the materials were books and magazines. To TJ, it was a secret coding system. He liked to pretend that he was a spy looking for a treasure located at these specific coordinates.

"Well, now Millie and TJ. You are both very familiar with the Dewey Decimal system. So, this is where you get to have fun! Let's see how many books you can find from your list. I will wait at the entrance to this room for you." Papa enjoyed presenting surprising yet educational challenges to Millie and TJ.

"Yay!" exclaimed the twins.

"Let's make a game of it!" exclaimed Millie. "Let's see who is able to find the most books on their list."

"Sure!" said TJ. "I have five books on my list including my comic book. How many are on your list?"

"Good question." said Millie. "I five as well."

"Then we are set." said TJ.

"Okay," said Papa. "Let's get started. You have 30 minutes to find your books. The clock starts, now." Off went the twins to search the catalogue and document the location of their books! Papa looked on with pride. Millie and TJ have been accustomed to using the library services since they were 3! He and Momma made it a point to teach them because they knew that knowledge is about comfort with information. Papa took a seat on the bench located at the entrance to the Children's Room. This bench was in place so that parents would have a full view of the room and the children

Millie and TJ continued with their search. Millie was not as concerned with winning as she was with finding the one most important book on her list. When she found it, Millie could not believe it! She froze for a moment. Then she saw TJ pass by and remembered that she was racing against TJ to find her books. Millie jumped up immediately and ran to find the other books!

Finally, Millie had all of her books. The stack was pretty large, but she managed to carry them toward the entrance. Millie had not paid any attention to TJ's whereabouts. She had almost forgotten, again, there was even a race until she heard TJ shout, "I won! I won! Papa I found my books faster than Millie!" Millie looked over her book stack and could see that TJ was already at the entrance with Papa! 'Oh, well', thought Millie, 'at least I have my most important book'. The twins headed to the front desk to checkout their books.

Once they arrived home, they immediately ran to the home library to place their books on their respective desks. Papa and Momma always requested that library books are placed on the desks and only one book at a time may be removed for reading. This was done to ensure no book was ever misplaced. Since they had started going to the library, Papa and Momma had created this manner of order. Because of this, neither Millie nor TJ have ever lost a library book.

"Wash your hands and you can have a snack." said Papa, "Then you either start on a book or play outdoors." Millie knew that she would start on her books. TJ, of course, wanted to hurry outdoors to play football with Michael, Jimmy and the rest of the neighborhood boys. The twins ran off to wash their hands.

By the time the twins had come back downstairs, Papa had the peanut butter and jelly sandwiches and cookies on the table. Millie's sandwich was just peanut butter as she did not enjoy jelly as much. TJ had both on his sandwich. "TJ, take your time! Your friends will still be outside when you get there!" Papa had to remind TJ to slow down. TJ just smiled between bites. He was in such a hurry to get outside with the hopes of being captain for the next round of plays.

As soon as he was done, TJ grabbed his jacket and headed out with Papa yelling behind him, "Don't leave this neighborhood and watch for the cars!"

"Yes, Sir!" TJ yelled over his shoulder as he closed the door. Millie nibbled on her cookie as she read through the first chapter of her top choice book. Once she was done with her cookies, Millie found a comfortable spot by the bay window in their home library and curled up for a good read.

Millie read until it was time for dinner and Momma had come home. TJ had already come indoors to get a head start on his comic book. TJ was sitting in the leather winged back chair reading a Marvel comic when Momma arrived.

"What, no hug for your hardworking Momma? Those adventures must be wonderful!" said Momma as she came into the library.

"Momma!" squealed the twins in unison as they ran to give Momma a hug. Momma worked some Saturdays as part of her rotation at the hospital. Millie and TJ really did not like having Momma away on Saturdays, but they understood the necessity. Besides, they had Papa!

"So, which books did you get?" asked Momma. "I found all of my books." said Millie.

"So did I! I even found them faster than Millie!" TJ announced with pride.

"Good for you, TJ! Did the list help?" TJ responded with great joy,

"It really did, Momma! It was much easier to select books when you have it written down." Momma was happy to hear that advanced preparation is seeing its way as an important tool for TJ and Millie to use in the future.

"Where is Papa?" asked Momma.

"He is upstairs replacing light bulbs for Mrs. Feathers." said Millie. Mable Feathers was an older woman who rented the apartment that the Jacobson's owned on the third floor. Marlene and Tyrone Jacobson purchased the three-story building as soon as they had gathered enough money after working multiple jobs through and after college. They immediately renovated the third floor to rent that unit. Their first tenants were Henry and Mable Feathers. They were a retired couple on a fixed income. Marlene and Tyrone loved having the Feathers around. They were very kind and often quiet. When Mr. Feathers passed away, Marlene and Tyrone assured Mrs. Feathers that she would not have to move. The Feathers did not have any children and they were like family to the Jacobson's.

Marlene headed up to Mrs. Feathers' apartment to see if she could be of help and to say hello. Tyrone was replacing the last bulb when Marlene knocked. "Come in." said Mrs. Feathers in such a sweet, inviting voice.

"Hi, Ms. Mable. Is Tyrone still here?"

"Yes, he is child. How was your day?" Ms. Mable responded as she hugged Marlene in her traditional manner of greeting family.

"I had a good day. The weather is perfect and all scheduled doctors were on shift today. Who can complain about that?" said Marlene. Marlene really enjoyed Ms. Mable's hugs. They reminded her of the hugs her grandmother would give her when she was a child. Ms. Mable took Marlene by the hand and led her into the living room where Tyrone was changing the final bulb.

"Hey, Sweetie!" exclaimed Tyrone as he dismounted the ladder to hug his wife.

"Hi, Babe!" responded Marlene as they embraced. Mable looked on in admiration. The Jacobson's had as much love as she and Henry. That is why Mable loved them so much. "I just wanted you to know that I am home. Do you need any help?" asked Marlene.

"Nope. Got it all under control. I thought that we would do a small barbecue today. Do you feel up to making your infamous potato salad?" Papa asked with a grin. He knew that Momma would not turn down a request from him with a smile.

"You are smooth. Of course I will make the salad. Just let me get out of this uniform. I will see you downstairs. Is the meat marinated?"

"It sure is." Papa grinned. Momma gave Ms. Mable a good-bye hug.

"You are joining us for dinner aren't you, Ms. Mable?"

"Of course, Dear!" Ms. Mable enjoyed spending time with the Jacobson's. It makes the nights so less lonely. Since Henry had passed, Ms. Mable had become that much more dependent on the Jacobson's. They remind her of the peace, laughter, and joy she had with Henry. Henry used to say that the Jacobson's are going places. He said that they have what it takes to rule the neighborhood if not the world! Momma headed downstairs. The twins were still reading in the library by the time she had changed and returned to the first floor of their home. "Millie, would you like to help me prepare potato salad for dinner?"

"Sure, Momma." Millie enjoyed helping Momma and Papa in the kitchen. It was like performing experiments like the ones Momma had read about from her science books. Millie had a strong interest in science and looked forward to becoming a doctor when she grew up.

Millie grabbed her apron from the hook in the kitchen and slid her step stool that Papa made for her over to the center island. Momma placed a bowl of potatoes on the island along with the potato peeler. Millie spread newspaper on the island top. The newspaper was for the collection of the potato peels. Millie

liked using the potato peeler. It made peeling the potato easy for her small hands. Once the salad was finished, Momma placed the bowl in the refrigerator so that it could chill and finalized the seasoning preparation of the meat. By this time, Papa and TJ were out on the deck preparing the grill. Once the grill was hot enough, Papa sent TJ in for the platter of meat.

Millie began setting the table for dinner. She remembered to set a place for Ms. Mable. It was a little sad not having a place setting for Mr. Henry. Millie did not understand what really happened to Mr. Henry. Momma and Papa said that Mr. Henry was ill and had been ill for quite some time. After a long time of being ill, he passed away. Millie figured that that was Papa and Momma's way of keeping she and TJ from asking too many questions that dealt with death. Anyway, Millie really liked Ms. Mable all the same and always tried to have something special for her whenever she came to dinner. This evening, Millie had made a card for Ms. Mable that had flowers and smiley faces on the cover. Millie placed the card next to Ms. Mable's plate.

Ms. Mable arrived with a picture of homemade lemonade. The Jacobson's enjoyed Ms. Mable's homemade lemonade. It had the right amount of sweet and tart. Everyone enjoyed dinner. This was to be the last barbecue for the season as it was starting to get a bit cool. Millie and TJ really liked barbecue dinners. There was a variety of meats to taste and eat and of course Ms. Mable's homemade lemonade!

Millie and TJ began clearing the table after dinner as Momma and Papa moved to the living room with Ms. Mable to talk about current events and the neighborhood activities. The Jacobson's made it a habit to discuss events on a regular basis. It was their way of staying abreast of politics and means to help with progress in their neighborhood. Over cups of coffee, Papa, Momma, and Ms. Mable talked about events and happenings in the neighborhood. Not too much has changed so they had conversations full of laughter and good memories of Mr. Henry.

TJ and Millie finished clearing the table and rinsing the dishes. They headed to the living room to say good night to the adults. After giving each a hug, TJ and Millie raced upstairs to put on their pajamas.

Millie and TJ were brushing their teeth when Momma and Papa had come up to tuck them into bed. "Look at these Babies, Momma. They are truly a Blessing" said Papa holding Momma around the waist as he did so often.

"Yes in deed." smiled Momma.

"But, I am not a Baby!" said TJ with a mouth full of paste. TJ did not enjoy the reference to "Baby". At the age of 9, TJ felt he is beyond being called a "Baby" even by Papa and Momma! Papa and Momma smiled in understanding. However, in their minds, TJ and Millie will always be their Babies.

TJ and Millie headed to their rooms with Papa and Momma behind them. Momma went to TJ's room first while Papa went to Millie's room. They then switched rooms leaving behind their final good night wishes and turning off the lights.

The following weeks went by very quickly. TJ and Millie would race home each weekday to hurry with their homework and studies so that they could get to their library books. Tomorrow is Saturday and the books were due back at the library! Finally, Saturday had arrived! TJ and Millie grabbed their book stack and waited for Papa. "Okay, my Geniuses, are you ready?" asked Papa.

"Yes!" exclaimed the twins in unison.

"Do you have all of your books?" asked Papa.

"Yes!" the twins exclaimed. "Do you have your library card?"

"Yes!" exclaimed TJ and showed Papa his wallet with his library card in the identification slot. Millie looked worried. She searched the books thoroughly and could not find her card. Millie's worry turned to heartbreak.

"What is wrong, Princess?" Papa asked with gentleness. He knew what the look meant. Tears began to slowly slide down Millie's face. She spoke slowly.

"Papa, I lost my library card. I am sure I placed it in my book as a bookmark each night and now it is not there." More tears streamed. TJ placed his arm around his sister's shoulders.

"It will be okay, Millie. We will find it." TJ spoke with such assurance that Millie really believed him. Papa agreed.

So, the search began. TJ searched the library; Millie searched her book bag; and Papa searched Millie's room. After 30 minutes of diligent searching, they reconvened in the home library. Millie still maintained a continence of sadness. Papa assured Millie that all would be well. Papa explained that although losing her library card is an unexpected event, she is permitted a free replacement at the local library. So they gathered their books and headed to the library.

What was once a beacon of excitement for Millie was now a looming presence of doom and embarrassment. Millie walked with heavy steps toward the building. She was not looking forward to having to tell Ms. Margaret that she had lost her card. Millie waited so long for the opportunity to get her very own card and now it was gone. Papa stopped to talk to Millie as TJ raced up the library steps. Papa and Millie sat on the steps. He placed his arm around her shoulders and pulled her close while speaking gently.

"Don't worry, Princess. Trust me. Everyone makes mistakes. The mistake is not what matters. What matters is the lesson learned and the actions we take to mitigate the opportunity to repeat our mistakes." Millie agreed with a slow nod of her head. They got up from where they sat and headed up the remaining steps toward the library doors. As Papa and Millie entered, Ms. Margaret could tell right away that all was not well. Millie approached the front desk with a heart as heavy as her steps.

Slowly, sliding her books toward Ms. Margaret, Millie said, "Good morning, Ms. Margaret. I am so sorry. I lost my library card and need a new card." Millie looked back at Papa to see if there was more she needed to say. Papa gave her a smile of assurance.

Ms. Margaret, realizing how very difficult this must be for Millie to admit, responded in a gentle tone, "It is not the end of the world Millie. Because this can happen to anyone, we offer a free replacement for the first time a subscriber looses or misplaces his or her card. However, additional cards will cost a fee. Please, take care as I am sure your parents respect the services we provide and would not enjoy having to pay extra." Millie nodded with understanding as she knew that Papa and Momma discussed budget and finance often at home. Ms. Margaret printed a new card for Millie and used that card to check her books back into the library stack.

Millie and TJ collected their new books for the month and headed home with Papa. Millie was careful to place her new library card in the front pocket of her jacket that had a zipper. Once they reach the house, Millie and TJ placed their books in the home library and headed upstairs to wash their hands for lunch. TJ was the first to reach the table after washing his hands. "Papa, I need a favor" said TJ.

"Sure, Little Man. What is the favor?"

"Papa, can you take me to the Five and Dime when Momma gets home? I need to get something that is very important. I am sure I have enough money." TJ said this as he reached into his pocket and pulled out the money that he had saved in his bank box. TJ kept money given to him as gifts that was in excess of the money he deposited into the savings account that Papa and Momma had opened for him. There was a separate account opened for Millie. Papa looked at the money and wondered what TJ was up to but agreed to the request. As soon as Momma arrived home, Papa and TJ left to run this secret errand. Papa let Momma know where they were going and that it was TJ's request. Momma was as curious as Papa, but trusting Papa agreed to the mission.

Once they arrived at the store, TJ headed straight to the department where they sold wallets and purses. He was dragging Papa along. Papa was beginning to figure out what TJ was up to. He smiled just thinking about TJ's intent. A sales woman approached TJ and asked, "Can I help you, Young Man?"

TJ looked her directly in the eyes and with confidence and clarity inquired, "Where can I find a wallet for a girl?" The sales woman guided TJ to a section of the store where there were small purses on display. They were purses just the right size for a girl. In a bin on the table right next to the purse carousel were wallets. TJ thanked the sales woman and began his search for wallets.

There were quite a few from which to choose. After searching for a while, TJ picked up a wallet and smiled as he examined the design and compartments. The wallet was perfect! It was red, Millie's favorite color, with three flowers and had identification slots just like the one TJ carries! TJ looked at Papa and exclaimed, "Papa! This is it! I have to get this for Millie! She can place her library card in here and not loose it! Papa! This is perfect!" Papa agreed. The wallet was a great idea and the design TJ chose really did fit Millie's personality. TJ and Papa made their way to the counter to pay for the wallet. TJ was so excited about having found the wallet that he had not taken the time to check the price tag to see if he had enough money. All that he knew was that he had found the perfect solution for Millie's situation.

"That will be $3.00." said the sales lady. TJ removed the money from his pocket and began counting what he had. To his surprise, TJ only had $2.00.

TJ looked worried. He did not want to ask Papa for the money. He wanted this to be his gift to Millie. Then TJ remembered something that Papa and Papa-Jacobs, Papa's father, had told him. They told him that a man would honor his word and work hard to obtain the necessities for himself and his family. TJ turned to Papa.

"Papa, I only have $2.00. I need $1.00. I want to know if I can borrow $1.00 from you and work around the house to pay you back?" Papa was impressed with TJ's quick thinking and honorable approach. He was so impressed that without hesitation he responded

"Yes. TJ that can be worked out." Papa handed a dollar to TJ. After paying, he and TJ headed back home for TJ to wrap his special gift for Millie. Once they arrived, TJ bolted to his room to wrap the gift. Papa sat at the table to have coffee with Momma and tell her about the adventure. Momma was very proud of TJ and agreed to keep the secret.

TJ locked his bedroom door so that Millie would not be able to walk in and catch him wrapping the surprise. He reached under his bed for the box of special papers he collected. Whenever TJ received gifts, he would save his favorite paper wrappings. He kept the wrappings in an old shoebox beneath his bed. TJ found some twine that he had managed to save from a package that Papa had once received. TJ loved the wallet. He carefully wrapped the wallet being sure to pull the small paper over all sides to hide it well enough. He secured the paper with the twine and sat back to examine his work. Picking up his wrapped surprise, TJ headed back downstairs.

When TJ entered the kitchen, Momma and Papa stopped talking and looked at him with a smile. TJ knew that Papa had told Momma and he did not mind. TJ placed the wrapped gift on the table at the place that Millie often sat. Then he approached Papa. "So, Papa, what kind of chores do you need me to do? Remember I still owe you $1.00." Papa looked at TJ and said, "Well, TJ, there is a lot of saw dust on the basement floor from my last workshop project. If you sweep that up, I think that will satisfy that $1.00 loan." TJ headed for the basement. Papa would not have normally been so easy on an opportunity like this. However, the repayment of the loan was to satisfy TJ's commitment to behave as a Jacobson man. But, the circumstance under which the loan was created more than paid his debt in full. TJ did not realize that his independent act of love and concern for his sister was a Jacobson Man act of responsibility.

By the time that TJ finished sweeping the sawdust, it was time to wash for dinner. Because TJ was so dusty, he had to take a bath. He knew that it was going to be a quick bath since he could smell the delicious aromas coming from the kitchen and knew that dinner was almost ready. After his bath, TJ set the table. Millie came down from her room when Momma called her. Millie gets so engrossed in her books that it is like she is transformed to another place. It takes a moment to break her concentration. TJ would often wish he had that same focus, as Papa and Momma called it. TJ enjoyed reading but not nearly as much as Millie.

When Millie sat down at the table, she noticed something wrapped at her place setting. Picking up the wrapped item, Millie carefully untied the twine. She could not believe it! The wallet was beautiful. "Oh my goodness!" Millie squealed!

"I brought it for you." TJ said with such pride. "It has a place for you to put your library card. Now, you won't loose it." Millie could not believe it. Her own wallet and a gift from TJ! She ran around the table and hugged TJ.

"Thank you, TJ! You're the best brother ever! I can't wait to put my library card in it! And it is my favorite color, red!" Millie hugged TJ, again. Right after dinner, Millie placed her library card in the wallet. At the same time, she wondered where had her first library card gone. That she may never know. But, what she did know was that she had a new wallet from a brother who was also her best Friend!

Printed in the United States
By Bookmasters